When Did You Find You?

WHEN DID YOU FIND YOU?

CHRIS DANIEL

INLOVE WITH WORDS MEDIA GROUP
HOUSTON

COPYRIGHT

Copyright © 2020 by Chris Daniel
All rights reserved. This book or any portion thereof may not be reproduced or used in any manner whatsoever without the express written permission of the publisher except for the use of brief quotations in a book review.

Printed in the United States of America

First Printing, 2020

ISBN 978-1-7358414-0-3

InLove with Words Media Group, LLC
7205 Almeda Road

P.O. Box 301086

Houston, TX 77230

www.inlovewithwords.org

DEDICATION PAGE

I want to first thank my Creator for giving me breath each day.

Next, I owe a great deal of gratitude to my mother, Barbara Ann Daniel. Although we do not always see eye to eye because of our similarities, your love has gotten me to this point. The wisdom you have instilled over the years walks with me daily.

Finally, to my wife, Jimasha, and kids, Trey, Bryceson, and Jaicee, I offer everything I have in my heart to you. Thank you all for believing in my vision even when I did not. I appreciate the fact that you loved me even when my internal frustrations where expressed in my behavior and mood. You all are the best support team ever!!!!!!!

My love for each of you runs deeper than you will ever know.

Contents

INTRODUCTION 1

HELP ME 14

DO YOU KNOW SUCCESS? 26

VICTORY 36

FAMILY REUNION 48

EPIPHANY 64

EVERYDAY 72

LATE NIGHT THOUGHTS 84

STAY FOCUSED 96

GRATITUDE 105
Author's Page 108

INTRODUCTION

Trying to think of the opening line for a book is probably one of the most nerve-racking events of a writer's life. The key is to ensure readers can build a connection with the words right off the bat. For ten years, I mentally abused myself trying to create a starting point. In my mind, the finished product was already visualized. There was just a severe case of failure to launch. The feeling was similar to seeing a good cook-book recipe but not going to the grocery store. My heart knew what was accomplishable, but my mind chose to focus on why it wouldn't work. I had to compromise with myself that my plan may be imperfect but action was necessary for it to develop.

Every morning I rose knowing it was the day to go all in and just start writing. Every morning I would find reason why it wasn't as important in real life as it was in my head. Every night I went to bed disappointed in myself for wasting my talent yet again. Day after day, I completed this routine until it became second nature. Over the years, I repeatedly heard one phrase- "You make time for what you want." It seemed as if everywhere I went, somebody was giving me that chunk of wisdom. After finally doing some self-reflecting, I realized my biggest barrier. Instead of making the book the primary focus, I directed all attention to why I couldn't complete it.

Being able to captivate people with my words has always been something that I touted myself as having great skill. During my elementary years, I knew my success would come from my voice. I can recall being in the fourth or fifth grade and participating in our Black History Month program. I can't remember any lines or even what character I was portraying, but I remember being on the stage during rehearsals. This was when I was first introduced to the diaphragm. Mrs. Woods would sit in the cafeteria's center, yelling, "I can't hear you! Speak from the bottom of your diaphragm!" This may be the reason I get those mean wife looks when she says I'm too loud. The joy I remember feeling from speaking was amazing. From that point on, I knew that I could get up and be a successful actor.

Unfortunately, that fearlessness that we possess as innocent children does not always last. As the years passed, change inevitably began to do its job. By the time middle school came, I was shopping in the husky section for clothes. It also did not help that my voice was trying to find itself. Out of nowhere, in the middle of conversation, my voice would switch octaves, pitch, and tone. Puberty. My comfort for being on the stage started to decrease more and more. Although my physical participation lessened, I was still engulfed in the skill of acting.

There was a sense of freedom in having the ability to put every piece of energy into portraying a character and leaving it all on the stage. I may not have known what being cathartic was in middle school, but I did understand the benefits. It was clear that I needed a way to get my thoughts out of my head at a young age. Growing up as an only child in a single-parent household allowed for a lot of solitary time with my mind. I did not have anyone to share my questions about life. And believe me, by seventh grade, I had a lot. Why do I only have one parent? Why do I have to wear glasses? What do I say to the cute girl at lunch? When I couldn't find the answers, I searched for them in the movies and shows I chose to watch.

It always amazed me that whichever mood was felt internally, there was something on television to support. I personalized my cinematic experience even more by learning to work the VCR. Future generations will never understand the luxury they have with all of their video-on-demand options. If there was a movie that I wanted to watch over and over, I would have to first start with the TV Guide. Whenever we went to the grocery store, the only purchases I requested were a TV Guide and blank VHS tapes. There was one that came with the Sunday newspaper, but it was something about actually buying a TV Guide that created excitement.

I would peruse that entertainment magazine thoroughly, marking my selections as I read. Once I had everything down that I wanted to watch, I would patiently wait for the time slot to arrive, pop in that blank tape, and hit record. I hadn't quite mastered the craft of setting the VCR to record yet. As my collection grew, I spent whatever free time I had studying the creations of Hollywood magic.

By the time high school rolled around, I was a ninja in the production room. I got to the point where I learned how to hook up two VCRs to record from one another. Yep, high technology.

I had built up the courage to get back on stage a couple of times but was never truly comfortable. It was around this time I start converting my passion for the screen to music. My mom was already letting me get music albums, actual vinyl, from the store. Prior to her permission, I was applying the same VCR recording skills to the audio cassette. Like every kid raised in the eighties and nineties, my mixtape collection began by recording whatever the radio was playing.

Listening to those cassette tapes helped me realized that music was equivalent to the freedom I witnessed on the big screen. The same stories I watched actors play out became customized screenplays in my mind when listening to music. While growing up, music was a constant factor in my life. My mother would always have something spinning on the record player. Music also let me know when her heart was heavy. She would go the piano that was owned by my late grandmother, Inez Virginia Bonney, and play *Battlefield for my Lord*. Being raised in the black church should create memories of this song. If not, be blessed to be in a day and age where it can simply be entered in a Google search. The pain I would hear from the pressing of those ivory keys let me know the release that music could create.

I was also engulfed with music through my uncle. During my childhood, he owned several nightclubs, and I was almost like his right-hand man. I can remember summers running errands with Uncle Jerry and making stops to check on the nightclubs. Since I was only eight or nine years old, I wasn't technically supposed to be in the building at all. Whenever we stopped, I had two locations to post up. Either sit in the back office where it stunk and smelled like sewage, or kick it in the DJ booth. I would always choose the latter when it was available. There were times when we would be there, and clearly, the happy hour rush was beginning. Whenever I was on my hideout mission in the booth, my only job was to keep the records coming. The area was not that big, so I would sit in a corner on the crates and keep handing vinyl to DJ John Justice (by the way, one of the coolest names I knew as a kid). This made me feel so important. Every now and then, I would peer out of the D.J. window to see this crowd of adults laughing, smiling, and dancing to the tunes. This was my second experience witnessing the power of music.

Of course, I am a product of the Hip-Hop generation, so storytelling means something truly special to me. To this day, I remember the first two hardcore, explicit albums I ever owned on a compact disc. Normally when my mom went record shopping, she would let me select something but never that 'gangster rap mess' as she would call it. The most explicit album in my portfolio was L.L. Cool J's *I'm Bad*. Don't get me wrong this was a great album, but definitely a different vibe from N.W.A. or Uncle Luke.

So, the first of the two was Scarface's *The Diary*. One of my mom's close friends gave me this album when I was around 13. I listened to each track faithfully every morning and night. If this album were to be played right now, I could easily go word for word with ninety-five percent. Before that, I was only able to hear the explicit versions when I visited my cousins. Ears that have not been blessed by this album and claim to be Hip-Hop aficionados are definitely short-changed.

Shortly after my receipt of this monumental album, I was given the green light to make my first ever CD purchase. My mom would always take weekly trips to music stores to purchase new records. I can remember it as clear as a bright spring day. We pulled up to Blockbuster Music, and the only reason we were here was for me to make my purchase. It felt so special. She didn't even get out of the car. She just gave me a $20 bill and let me be free. I walked right in those doors and went straight to the Hip-Hop/Rap section.

The selections seemed so infinite. There were so many artists, so many albums cover. They were all enticing. I had so many songs that I heard on the radio but had no clue what it took to pick a great album. There was one song that definitely stood out more than any other to my native Houstonian ears. *Swangin' & Bangin'* by E.S.G. Any residence of Houston during the mid-nineties knows this song flooded the airwaves. As far as Houston music goes, I think it may have only fallen second to Scarface's *I Seen a Man Die* at the time. There was no doubt in my mind that this had to be my first purchase.

During this time, Houston music was on the rise thanks to the incomparable Robert Earl Davis or, more commonly known, D.J. Screw. After constantly infusing my brain with the lyrics from Scarface and E.S.G., I was sold on the fact the no one could create a story better than a Houston rapper. Across the street from me were my two closest friends growing up, Will and Derrick. They both were older than me by a couple of years, but they took me under their wings. They were always listening to something, but both had extremely different tastes in music. Derrick chose to listen to music that had more of an upbeat, make the body move type of vibe. His CD collection included the likes of *The Score*, *When Disaster Strikes*, and *Anuthatantrum*. Will, on the other hand, was listening to more local, underground artists like Street Military, Fakkulty, and Botany Boys.

Although they were polar opposites when it came to music selection, one thing that bound us was DJ Screw. We would pile up in either the green Ford Explorer or the brown Buick Regal that Will's parents owned. Every Thursday night at 8:00, we made sure we were at DJ Screw's house waiting on that gate to open. We would all go with $20 to get two tapes each. The gate would open, and there would be a flood of people exiting their vehicles. The key goal was to always be in the front of the line to get prime selection. Once he was out of a particular dub, that was it. Another attempt would have to be made the next Thursday for that copy. Standing at that side door requesting tapes from Screw through his burglar barred door did not seem monumental at the time. We were just trying to get access to good music. Now looking back, I realize that experience was a great part of Houston music history.

After our purchases were complete, we would ride around listening to music that expanded far beyond our city limits. Remember, I am a storytelling student, and that is exactly what Screw did with his cassettes. He would take the soul on a journey through music at a pace where the only option was to vibe with the groove. The most special part of any Screw tape would be the instrumental moments when he let the beat just ride. It was in these moments I realized my talent for word use.

Whenever DJ Screw allowed the music to just go, it was almost guaranteed that one of the Screwed Up Click artists would get on and start freestyle rapping. This means creating songs on the fly with no written lyrics, for those outside of the Hip-Hop community. This inspired everyone who laid ears to the music to follow suit. During my high school years, everybody from Houston thought they were an aspiring rapper. I was not left out of this group. Whenever I was riding in the car with Will and Derrick, we would crank up the music and complete a cipher session. Every time I would open my mouth to speak, those cathartic feelings began to emerge again.

Until her recent, more elderly years, my Mom was always a fan of game rooms and casinos. She was always quick to hop on a bus with a group and ride to Louisiana to gamble. Those moments gave me the opportune time to hone in on my verbal skills. As soon as the coast was clear, Derrick and Will would come over, and I would pull out all the vinyl I could find. There was a large number of records that would always have an instrumental or two on the album. We would sit and try to recreate the energy that we would always hear in those Screw tape freestyle sessions.

Derrick was always there to be there, but Will and I would turn it into a competition. We would go back and forth with each other trying to invent better lyrics than the last. This was when I knew for sure that I had a talent with words. I would try to make it my goal to ensure no matter what I said, there was a story being told. The more sessions we had, the more confident I became in what I was saying. I started to open up outside of the trio and rapping amongst other friends and family members. Although my belief in my lyrics increased, I still didn't dare to be a performer on the big stage. I would limit my lyricism to certain groups of people. If there was a random cipher going with people I barely knew, I would not jump in at all. However, my ear was always active. I would listen to different styles of delivery and incorporate them into my technique.

The concept of writing down my lyrics never crossed my mind.

Sitting in my mama's living room freestyling over some old records was just something we were doing. No one had aspirations to be a rapper. We were just finding a way to kick back and have fun. It was quite therapeutic for me. This was my method of expressing my adolescent thoughts.

When I was younger, I remember finding an old journal that belonged to my grandmother, Inez. This journal included quotes and poems that she had written and collected over a period of time. She passed away when I was six, but I spent my entire childhood trying to connect with her based on the faint memories. In my heart, I felt and still feel that my talent for words was her last request for God to give me. As I began the attempt to understand my purpose with words, my mind naturally began reflecting. Much of what I uncovered began to come out in my freestyles. I can remember times I would be in a zone, and the release of pain would be so intense that tears could not resist. This was when I started thinking of myself as more of a poet. The funny thing was, I had never written any style of poetry unless it was an assignment in English class. I began telling myself any thought that entered my mind had to immediately get written on any nearby scrap piece of paper. That seemed so corny to me. In my mind, there was a huge difference between purging out my thoughts verbally and writing them. Due to my unwillingness to be free on the paper, everything I wrote sounded like the music that got the most radio play. All of my substance was completely materialistic and surface. This was a full reversal of everything I represented or valued. To this day, I refuse to listen to mainstream radio for my musical desires. Needless to say, I did not put forth an intense effort to fuel my purpose.

As time flew, I focused my energy on the expected path of the ordinary. I went to college. I was not built to be a traditional in the classroom, learning type of student (I now realize that 20 years and 2 degrees later). Rather, my education comes naturally from life experiences and not based on how well I can critique an article. I was still dabbling with my words and even getting in the studio with impressed friends. I had so many tell me that I should be pursuing music full-time, but I would always say school is my focus. The truth is that the fear of being placed at center stage as a performer still made me uneasy.

I remember the moment when it all clicked for me. The year was 2002. All I kept hearing was spoken word this and spoken word that. Now anyone between the ages of 14-40 during the mid-nineties was well aware of a comedy show by the name of *Russell Simmons' Def Comedy Jam*. I watched that show faithfully every Friday night at 11:00 pm. So, it only felt natural to tune in when I heard Russel Simmons was coming back with a reboot swapping comedy for poetry.

Russel Simmons Def Poetry Jam. I was hooked from the moment I witnessed the trailer for the show. Although I played with my words and freestyled as a hobby, I still was not a poet. At least, I didn't think.

When the first episode aired, I was in complete awe. It wasn't until then when I understood the true definition of poetry. My mental image of a poet was either some Black elder with salt and pepper hair or a twenty-something with tinted glasses walking around with burning incense. Now in the world of poetry, those images exist, but there is so much more beauty. On this show, there was a wide range of artists there all to serve one purpose, deliver their story through their words.

Seeing this eclectic group of performers placed a fire under me that mirrored being in those elementary school plays. I began flirting with the idea of getting back on stage. It started by just attending local open mics and blending into the audience. The vibe at these events created energetic peace. I left out every time feeling more motivated to respect my own words. By the end of *Def Poetry Jam's* run on television, I had built up a couple of notebooks of my own words.

The confidence I found from *Def Poetry Jam* and attending these open mics gave me the energy needed to shift from audience member to stage participant. The vibe reciprocated from the crowd confirmed that my purpose on Earth is sewn deeply in my words. As years passed and more tablets got inked, it was only natural to begin sharing with the world why God placed me here. This book is composed of just a few of the poems I have penned over time. These poems represent conversations I had with the Lord about my pursuance of fulfilling my purpose. Everyone has a reason for their life. Many know why immediately, and others have to dig to discover. As the words on the following pages are received, I hope that my journey will be the fuel needed for someone's spiritual vehicle.

HELP ME

As much as we say we may want to,

We cannot walk through this life alone.

There will be moments

When your body and soul will not be strong,

Strong enough to hold on.

You must connect with someone

Who can help you along.

Where we begin to go wrong

Chris Daniel

Is that our trust and faith

Are being less and less shown.

We feel that we should only focus on our own.

It is not our fault or concern

Of what goes on in someone else's home.

Everyone is busy chasing their personal throne,

Not the peace and tranquility of the Kingdom zone.

What has driven us away

From being concerned for fellow humans?

How we treat others has a heavy influence

On our pursuance of forward movement.

We must change our mental viewing

WHEN DID YOU FIND YOU?

Into something that is more congruent

To the lifestyle we should be using.

Instead, what seems to flow so fluent

Through our societal unit

Is, I've done it, why can't you do it.

Not, let me help you through it.

We feel that if others get to moving

They will overshadow all of our improvement

Why are we so clueless?

Not realizing that when others succeed

It is partially our doing by being an influence.

We rather listen to voices start spewing

Chris Daniel

Most of which sounds extremely foolish.

You only listen because your faith has become lucid.

Your pure thoughts are now diluted

With the notions and ideas

that evil has been producing,

Creating allusions and illusions

That brings nothing but confusion

To the gambit of solutions

You could be choosing.

Since your mind is now fusion

With evil inclusions

The original purpose of your plan begins eluding

WHEN DID YOU FIND YOU?

You might need to step back,

Do a little regrouping

So those thoughts that continue looping

Can get to moving.

This is not always possible thru solo viewing.

The clouds and fog

Won't allow you to see what you are doing.

All you can rely on

Are the voices those around you are using.

If those voices don't sound like progressive music

Do everything to remove them

From the process of your soul renewing.

Chris Daniel

Everybody isn't for you

And some find your failures amusing.

Your composure, you can't start losing.

Just constantly say to yourself

That you are refusing

To ignore your true usage.

If you have to swallow your pride

And ask for help, that's what you will be doing.

There was a time and place when questioning myself seemed like the thing to do. In all honesty, the growth out of that phase is still under construction. At the time of writing the previous piece, there were tons of changes occurring in my life that I had no clue how to handle.

I was a week away from my baby girl being born. I was now a fiancé. My firstborn was nearing two years old, and my manual to be a stepfather to a pre-teen hadn't arrived yet. I was lost.

Growing up without a father wasn't a big deal to me until it became a big deal. As I now stood in my place as a father, I did not feel equipped. I also felt as if I lacked any time to prepare. Becoming a father of someone else's child raised so many internal questions.

Had his biological father been an absent figure, the transition may have been a little smoother. That was not my scenario. My oldest admired his father to death, and there could never be a duplicate. He made that known very well. Whenever we would have conversations, he would insert his dad's philosophy. I know that it was just innocent admiration of a parent, but it created so much mental discomfort at the time. My inner focus became how do I minimize exposing my flaws rather than highlighting my attributes.

This transition into the family leader role was also skewed because my future wife was now working on her second marriage. When I met my wife, she was on the tail end of matrimony going sour. This was the first experience my oldest had with having a stepparent. From my perspective, he was not healthy at all for what they needed in life. There was a presence of verbal, mental, and, eventually, physical abuse. That was the straw that broke the camel's back. Somehow God knew that the time to interject me into their lives was at that moment. It is funny how I have never doubted the purpose behind our connection. I did, however, doubt my worthiness of this blessing.

I was stuck in the middle of this idolized father that my oldest had and this monster of an ex-husband that my fiancé had encountered (I must make sure that it is clear the two were different individuals). I wanted to make sure that the image I was giving my oldest would be one that could be respected and revered like his biological father. For my wife, I wanted to ensure her safety and let her know that she would never have to worry about mistreatment from me.

Although this is naturally the type of person I am, I got lost in my mind's perceived images. I focused so much energy on not being or being them that I stopped being myself.

There was always a fear of my true self not being approved. This is not to say that I was walking through our relationship, putting on a façade. It was more of a pressure I placed on myself to show that I can be good enough. If my wife and I had disagreements, I had to make sure I refrained from getting too animated or loud. Those who know me know that my voice is heavy and naturally boisterous.

I never wanted her to see me as a threat. If my oldest and I were having a conversation about sports, I would try my hardest to engage actively. This would be despite my lack of in-depth knowledge of the sports world.

The more I chose to sit with this fear of true exposure, the angrier I became.

By the time my biological children were born, I was

completely torn. I had no other option but to be my natural self with them.

They had no other fatherly images to relate to other than myself. I felt comfortable being my natural goofy, reflective self. This comfort was not an easy shift to deliver to my wife and oldest.

My anger began to sit deep within.

The anger was with myself, but would passive-aggressively be acted out towards my wife and oldest. It became intense for me because it seemed as if I had everything stacked against my success. I felt as if I had to prove myself on so many different levels.

I was the polar opposite of what I felt my family's image of a man should be. I have always enjoyed sports but was never a ride or die, have to be in front of the TV for every game kind of fan. I was not an abusive, demeaning type of man. It was just me.

I love music.

I have a sensitive outlook on life.

I do not demand power to earn respect.

I try to treat everyone with fairness.

Me.

I needed help but was not sure of how to go about asking. I honestly did not know the area that most needed help. I just knew that this anger and tension could not continue to live within. My hesitation to be vulnerable made it extremely difficult to seek outside assistance. It was best for me to start looking inward to discover who I needed to be. I have always been a firm believer in the power of God. When I lost my relationship with myself, I also lost my connection with God. He was me, and I no longer knew me; it made it difficult to know Him.

As I started back having conversations with God, the dialogue would continue to tell me to make time for my peace. I was spending so much time throughout each day trying to make the world pleasant for everyone else but myself. I needed to get back to doing something that brought clarity and purpose to my thinking. This was when meditation started to become a part of my life.

Never had I sat down in complete silence and managed my thinking. I've been in silence before, but it was complete mental chaos. Learning the importance of mindfulness became everything to me. I began understanding the need to be centered and balanced. Every morning we wake with a choice to make. Whether to hit the snooze button, what we are eating for breakfast, which outfit are we going to wear? Out of every choice made, one must ask themselves, will it throw off my balance? Or put my peace at risk?

Whenever a goal is being set to accomplish something in

life, these questions must be asked. If being overweight leads to frustration and eating right begins, will that cookie disrupt the peace being sought? If the goal is to gain a promotion at work, will being lackadaisical reach the desired results? Most of the time, goals and peace are intertwined. The only reason goals are even set is to attain something that will bring happiness, freedom, or both. When either of the two is achieved, peace and balance are gained.

I tried watching all types of YouTube videos and apps to help me locate my center. In the beginning, it was completely weird, and I would instinctively create a mental barrier. During my meditation, I would go through the motions, but the entire time would tell myself how pointless it all seemed. Anyone that has practiced mindful reflection knows that it is all about focusing on the breath. Doing that would create so much anxiety for me. As I would listen to the guided meditator, I would try to keep with their rhythm of breath and not my own. Once again, I was trying to live up to fabricated expectations I thought others needed from me. This led to my frustration, thinking I was doing it all wrong.

I was intent on this working. One day my epiphany moment came. I remember the point when I asked myself, "why are you scared to be vulnerable with yourself?" I came out of this mediation session with tears in my eyes. If I couldn't be honest with myself about accepting the pain, how could I expect anyone else? I began realizing that my constant worry about being the man my family needed me to be was stemmed from the lack of preparation I received. Not growing up with a man in the household left me with many unanswered questions as an adult. Now the time had come where I better have those answers. I did not know what to put on my scantron, I was just filling in bubbles.

When I began to dig deep into that pain, I was blessed with clarity. I took all of those dynamics that caused anger and pain in my life due to the lack of a father and started putting energy in not following the trend. I may not have known the right or wrong things to do, but I knew what caused me pain, and I did not want to mirror those practices. It was never about how I compared to the other men my family had experienced. It was always about what type of man I could be for them. Once I could be vulnerable with myself, I learned how to live comfortably in my flaws, among others.

DO YOU KNOW SUCCESS?

Seems like when your mind, body, and soul

Are in a position to succeed

The LORD will take heed

To everything, those 3 components need to proceed

All that is asked in return

Is to have the ability to receive and believe

That through all of your ups and downs

Keep steady focus, and your blessings will soon be seen

But the mistake that most frequently intervenes

We get frustrated with the scene we're seeing

Thinking everything is going to be the icing on the cake

And peaches and cream

The only question I have to that is

"If you never know disappointment

How will you know you're succeeding?"

Throughout my childhood, I only had one goal—be successful. I was not quite sure what it looked like or what I would be doing. All I knew was that I had to be successful. I remember moments when that inevitable question was asked to me as a child. "What do you want to be when you grow up?" I could never come up with an answer that seemed socially sufficient.

Doctor? No, I hated the sight of blood and needles. Lawyer? No. I couldn't imagine myself defending someone guilty or prosecuting someone innocent. Fireman? Next. Police officer? Hell no!! Teacher? No. I watched too many of my family members live in that profession only to have nothing at the end of it. They are also one of the most undervalued, underappreciated category of workers.

Life has a way of providing its ironic moments. For nearly two decades of my life, I have been working in education. It was not due to the pursuit. It was all just happenstance. I was in my last semester of college with no clue of a career. Someone told me they were hiring for teacher assistants at their school. I applied, got the job, and here I am one and a half decades later. Throughout my entire career, I have been silently telling myself that this is not forever. However, comfort started to develop.

Prior to working in the classroom, my job list was quite extensive. I had been everything from a security guard to an assembly line worker at a coffee plant to working in a retail store. My focus to do something big began to fade once I got a couple of years of comfort under me in the classroom. Summers off. Consistent paycheck. Concrete hours. It was the life.

I do not want it to get misconstrued, I have enjoyed every bit of my work in education. The changes that I have made in children's lives will always hit me in my heart. I always felt that being in the classroom was not the best way to serve them. Not because I was a terrible teacher. It was more so my lack of passion for teaching. I was not the most intellectual of students by the time my high school and college years rolled around. This was not due to an absence of intelligence but a deficiency in motivation.

There was nothing that intrigued me about being in the classroom. I loved to learn just not what they were teaching.

Anyone who has ever seen me in action in the classroom can attest to the fact that I was not the traditional teacher. I tried to encourage my students to think outside of the box. My first two years of teaching was done at an alternative school for students who were disciplinary problems. I was 23 years old and not dedicated to being an educator. Remember, at the time, it was just a job I found. I did not have a desire to sit down and create lesson plans. I could not see the need for preparation. I would just focus on my topic, go into each class, and wing it. Once the educational system has applied its grasp, especially with this demographic of students, your heart begins to open. I noticed how much society looked down on these students just because of their mistakes. I understood that they did something wrong, but these were just teenagers.

I tried to make it my mission to make school enjoyable for them. Since I was dealing with students who did not typically adhere to a traditional school, I decided to take several unorthodox routes. Of all subjects to have me teach, they started me out with 8th grade math. This was probably the maximum extent of my mathematical expertise. I can recall one day when I was trying to teach something but kept hearing finger snaps from the room's rear. When my eyes finally viewed what was occurring, they discovered there was a full-on dice game in the middle of my lesson. Rather than taking the traditional route by causing a scene and kicking the students out, I decided to join them. I invited the entire class over to watch the dice game. From there, I began an impromptu lesson about the functions of probability. Before I knew it, students were creating hypotheses of each shooter's chances to hit their point.

One of my most successful lessons was metric conversions. Many of my students were sent to this school for one of two things—fighting or drugs. When it came to metric conversions, I decided to use the knowledge most of them already possessed about drugs. When I initially introduced the subject, I just kept it straight from the textbook.

I could easily see the confused faces as I went through the steps of multiplication and division to convert. That is when I called on one student who was always verbally proud of his street pharmaceutical entrepreneurial endeavors. I asked him quickly, "how many grams are in an ounce of weed?" He replied just as quickly "28". I then hit him with my follow up question, "how many ounces are in a pound?" This time he replied with a little backup from other classmates, "16!!!!". I immediately let them know they just did their first metric conversion.

The sense of pride and accomplishment that sat on their faces was priceless. The lesson went as smooth as butter moving forward. It was at that moment I witnessed what it meant to be grateful. Every other educator these students encountered dismissed them immediately because of their background or behavior. They were instantly viewed as their actions and not of them. When I saw them, I saw myself at that age, trying to figure life out. There was no lack of education in their lives, just the absence of compassion. The respect I earned from these students came solely from them knowing I recognized them as a breathing person and not a numerical statistic. Going through the steps of life can be difficult. Getting knocked down is a possibility. The key is not to focus on the knockdown but to enjoy the journey of getting up. There is so much time spent focusing on the world's problems we forget the beauty it truly possesses.

My life observations have concluded we focus more on the fall than the getup because of our societal systems. Take something as simple as a baby or a toddler falling on the floor. Everyone around them is quick to the rescue no matter how hard or soft the fall. Most babies will not start crying until panic and immediate rush ensue. They do not know that pain is supposed to bother them. Sit back and watch that same baby from a distance. They will rub their head, stop to figure out what happened, and keep moving. This skill gets lost with age. This philosophy should be carried through life.

Instead of crying and complaining about what has happened, just acknowledge it and keep onward.

The problem is the grind gets far less attention than the mistakes. This is not to say there is disrespect in the grind, but some may lack understanding. We all recognize mistakes regardless of what arena created them. Errors remind us of the pain that we have endured at some point in our own personal journey. When people see others hurting, they want to rush to take care of the problem. The ones who are glad to see the pain in others will reveal their happiness one way or another. Every human being desires the need to be noticed. Everyone wants some level of attention. When working in the trenches doing the dirty work, fewer people will give the attention individuals typically crave. This is the perfect time to reevaluate the dynamics of the support circle. Who are the people willing to support wholeheartedly throughout the grind? Who is just waiting on the sidelines to witness mistakes to occur? This is when the internal question must be asked of the 'who' and 'why.' Who are the goals being chased for? Why are they worth achieving? At the end of self-reflection, it should be easier to narrow down the people whose opinions matter.

By asking these questions to myself, I realized my journey on this path was for everyone but myself. I had my mother and late grandmother that I wanted to make proud. They valued education deeply and believed that no success would be granted if a degree went unearned. I wanted to be a motivator for all of my friends who gave up on education along the way. When I was fresh out of high school, I had many friends and family members that started their collegiate journey alongside me. By the time I got to the end, I looked up and realized that I was the only one still enduring. The mentality my mother instilled in me about the importance of college began to play with my mental outlook towards my friends.

I began feeling heavy levels of discomfort being in my circles. The story I began creating was that I was developing a sense of misalignment with them. This was not to say I was feeling better than anyone or arrogant. This was more naivety thinking that education had the same importance to everyone as it did to me. It didn't feel right talking about enlightened thoughts I had with classmates with my circle who was no longer seeking that level of knowledge.

The other dilemma created was my lack of desire to develop friendship/support circles at my new level. There were tons of factors surrounding my reasoning. I did not want my family and friends to feel abandoned by me. I was comfortable in the lifestyle we had.

Going out to parties, getting drunk, acting irresponsibly was a bond that we built together. This is where I felt I belonged. On the flip side, I knew that I wanted to better myself through education. However, I didn't feel worthy of being in the circle of academia. I did not take learning as seriously as I should, and when I heard the collegiate conversations that occurred, I felt intimidated. I was stuck right in the middle. I was beyond the party-all-the-time lifestyle but did not feel adequate enough to be in the scholastic arena.

My stubbornness to make the proper adjustments led me to just move through life on average mode. It sunk me into a shell that would not be cracked until more than a decade later. I had to start learning to ask myself when I was going to begin doing it for me. When was I going to start chasing the goals I truly wanted to pursue? It was beginning to get more difficult to chase my dreams based on what I needed rather than the made-up expectations I thought others had for me.

As I began my journey through mindfulness, it became clear to me many of the goals I had accomplished in life. I learned to start making my achievements primary rather than my inadequacies. In doing this, I realized how important it is to not try to fit into a circle. We are all born with unique traits and characteristics. When life begins to revolve around those individualities, the correct circle begins to form. When studying the 'greats' of the past, regardless of profession, there came a time when they had to isolate and do what was best for their purpose.

Practicing mindfulness definitely helped me realize that all of the fears and doubts within were all self-inflicted. This is why we must be careful with what we say to ourselves. There is no ability to control which thoughts enter the mind.

The primary function of the mind is to think. The only control individuals have is which thoughts are going to be allowed to linger. Everyone can let go of thoughts no matter how heavy. I made it my mission to praise every success, whether big or small, mentally. Doing this with consistency allowed me to notice the false expectations that I had previously been setting.

VICTORY

We will all one day grow old

We will all have to face

That day when our clock

No longer tocks

As I look back thru my life

I wonder if I have done enough

Are my efforts sufficient?

Because presently

CHRIS DANIEL

I don't have that feeling

If tomorrow were not mine

Would the ones I leave behind be fine?

Because I have been walking

Thru this world, blind

Standing instead of fighting

To get to the front of the line

With a single thought saying be patient

God takes time

Yeah, but I don't' think

It was His design

For me to just stare

WHEN DID YOU FIND YOU?

At the back of someone's head

In this "I Have a Dream" line

Wishing Dr. King was here

Maybe black folks would have it better this year

Nah, I think God would rather me

Breakout of this line

To perform actions

That invoke fear

In anyone who stands in front

Of what He has made clear

I am here to speak words into ears

But before that, I must grab my shield and spear

Chris Daniel

And prepare for battle with the demons

That are trying to control me

Saying remember the old me

The reckless, carefree, fun me

Partying all the time

No schedule to keep

But I try to tell them

My life is different now

That is no longer what is best for me

Those pastimes were the times

When my mind was truly confined

And I couldn't get these words past my teeth

WHEN DID YOU FIND YOU?

So, I beg you to set me free

And this is the last time I will ask politely

The next time it will be my feet

Walking all over you in defeat

As I yell to the top of my lungs, VICTORY

There has to come a time when a stance is made to stop thinking about it and do something. Most people who do not reach their pinnacle of success is not because they lack ideas.

Their success never comes to fruition because they fail to take action. I was once an avid member of this group and still attend random meetings. No matter how great my ideas are, I somehow create a method for procrastinating. I have tried setting concrete goals and timelines for myself. My error was assuming that somehow the right words would just hit me in the middle of the night.

There are two types of action that one can take towards something. Passive or active action. Both can be self-fulfilling but only one will actually produce results. This book has been in the stage of passive action for years. The information presented on these pages should have been provided to the world years ago. I have set deadline after deadline for when it needed to be finished but continued to function out of passive action.

What is passive action? This is when most people are in the developing phase of their dream. This is what helps to get the inspiration flowing. The problem begins to develop when we get stuck and complacent. In preparation for this book, time was spent researching everything needed to become an author. How to become self-published? How to get copyrighted? Anytime there was a spoken word event, I would try to be there. I just knew if I engulfed myself in the writing community, I would vicariously begin to be an author.

Don't get me wrong. Every aspiring author needs to follow similar steps in order to aid them in becoming a success. My steps turned into passive action because I never put words on paper at the end of the day. I would never force myself to sit and actually write. My writing would come on a whim or when I felt like it. This was passive action. I took all of the steps to start writing the book but never took the most crucial one. Start writing.

Have you ever met someone who constantly talks about big dreams, but they continue to remain in the same spot? Passive action. There are many reasons why we get stuck at this level. Some are legit and are based on uncontrollable obstacles that arise.

The other reasons are just tales we mentally create to support our lack of moving forward. Creating these stories makes us feels good about being stuck. This gives us a reason to place the blame elsewhere for stagnation rather than looking inward. It is much easier to say that external factors have delayed progress than to admit inner fears are the true culprit.

Passive action derives from the doubt that lies within. It is that little voice in the mind concentrating on every hindrance that may occur. Exerting energy towards barriers that may impact goals is natural in the process, but they should never remain present. All problems have a solution. It just needs to be determined how bad the desire is to really get it solved.

Active action, on the contrary, is the path to freedom. Think of someone building a house from the ground up. It takes many steps before building can commence.

The land must be acquired. Next, a builder must be sought. Obtain permits and secure financing. Create the blueprint. I could go on and on. It doesn't become real until a shovel is placed in the dirt to start building. This is active action. It is the moment when talking stops, and implementing the plan actually starts. This is the only way to get closer to the end goal.

The only difference between passive and active action is one step. Get moving. All of the steps needed before building that house can become passive by allowing obstacles to stop forward movement. Time does not allow us the luxury of letting our actions become passive. Time is guaranteed to be gone once it is gone. There has always been a point in life when the perception was there is no need to rush because time will be available later.

Typically, when waiting for later, space is allowed for more obstacles to mature. In order not to get stuck, the acquisition of solid time management skills is vital. As mentioned earlier, 'you make time for what you want.' When consumed in the process of goal setting, time must be allotted for needs over wants. Yes, it feels good to sit and binge-watch that new hot topic show. The internal reflection that must be addressed is tied to the feelings that arise once the show is over. Did that elapsed time help bring the goal closer? If that pit of incompletion sits in the stomach region, it is time to reevaluate how each minute of the day is spent.

For this reevaluation to occur, one must honestly observe themselves. I challenge each reader to spend one day journaling hour by hour what their day looked like. This does not have to be anything elaborate. Just tear out a sheet of paper and place it somewhere it can constantly be seen. From the morning's waking moments to the nightly shutdown, record each hour what was accomplished for the day. Regardless if that hour was spent cooking, scrolling through social media, or just daydreaming, record it.

Writing allows thoughts the freedom to roam outside of the head and make them tangible.

Now that wasted time can be visualized, the process of elimination must begin. The list should not be heavily imbalanced with distractions over the actual grind. Itemization will help build more conscience of what encourages yearning to get off track. Everything should now be placed into perspective for those who have been in passive action with their goals. It is amazing how much time gets squandered just because we fail to self-discipline.

After the list has been dissolved into only essential actions, a schedule must be created. A solid planning system is needed to help establish a concrete strategy. Many people have resorted to downloading some type of electronic application to help them organize their schedules. Nothing is more powerful than the presence of pen and paper. Technology is good to use on the go, but it can become a liability when truly attempting to dig deep. How many times does the initial purpose of using a phone or computer for serious business result in getting trapped in a wormhole of distractions? It starts with opening the productivity app of choice. Next, it moves to checking a couple of emails, then to responding to text messages, and finally, on to learn what's trending. In order to create accountability, there must be a tangible item to grasp. Having a binder, journal, planner, or anything similar limits the intercepting distractions. It is clear that it can only be used for its designed purpose.

The next step is to create a space that is dedicated only to the grind. I did not understand how important this was until I finally formed my office space. In all of the years I have been in my house, I kept saying that I would turn our extra room into my Zen. I allowed that thought to turn into passive action. It had become everything but my workspace. This was always my primary reason for not being able to creatively grow into becoming an author.

I would sit in the main room to write but constantly complained about everyone interrupting my thoughts. I tried going to coffee shops and bookstores for peace and solitude but would easily find interferences there. The come and go of people would not allow me to go into my thoughts comfortably. When I finally dedicated the time to go into that extra room and create space for my goals, progress started to appear. I finally had a safe area for me to lock in and concentrate. If the primary vice is being easily susceptible to distractions, this is a non-negotiable.

Now that the tasks have been planned out and an isolated space of productivity is prepared, there is one more requirement. Continuously acknowledge and celebrate personal accomplishments regardless of how large or small. Remember, when creating something, barriers are inevitable. There is no doubt they will appear. This is why every time a goal gets accomplished, it must be recognized. It can be something as simple as waking up when eyes first open. That needs to be commended. Showing self-gratitude acknowledges that it can be done and creates inspiration to do it again. The natural inclination should be to shift behaviors that will manifest greatness and move the goal closer.

FAMILY REUNION

What stops us from moving

When nothing is preventing us from moving

I have come to the conclusion

That it must be the confusion of delusions

That our minds are constantly producing

That provides this stagnation of movement.

Our minds can hinder or help

Depending on which part we are using

But it seems a tad bit confusing

Chris Daniel

That after all of the bumps and bruising

We continue on paths we should not be pursuing.

The first delusion of confusion is that of fear.

Fear is used to prevent progress

As long as there is fear

No one can produce their best

The history books put that theory to test.

Had our civil rights leaders had fear

We would still be riding buses from the rear

Or facing spray hoses and dog's year after year

Fear can be contagious to those it comes near

Puts questions in minds from words caught by the ear.

WHEN DID YOU FIND YOU?

Someone could have the brightest plan

But allow fear to tell them there is no chance

Because of what interfered with someone else's plan.

Once fear accomplishes his mission

He brings aboard his cousin from a distance.

And this cousin has a familiar recognition.

There is some point

When we have used his words for description

This cousin goes by the name of doubt

And he can't wait for fear to get settled

So, he can begin coming out of our mouths.

Because fear would never hold complete ground

Chris Daniel

If doubt never came around

Fear is the emotion

That gives doubt justification to be spoken aloud

It can be spoken individually or amidst a large crowd.

Doubt holds the reason for fear

And diminishes the plan to persevere

Many have succeeded with fear

Learning to deal with it

Using it to continue shifting gears

When fears begin to couple with doubt

thoughts of endurance get knocked right out.

Doubt tells those who accept him

WHEN DID YOU FIND YOU?

That they are not worthy

Incapable of being a better person

There were times when I was this person

Until I realized the dynamics of this familial coercion

This is why certain people can never evolve

Elements of doubt and fear have never dissolved

This can't be the philosophy we continue to revolve

I figured out a plan to get this family reunion resolved

I will continue to uplift and support the rest of y'all

That have been stuck between these walls

Because the only way to stand

Is to get up from the fall

We are now delving into factors that play an important role in goals going unaccomplished. These characteristics have, at some point, been experienced by every human being breathing. No one holds any immunity. I am talking about fear and doubt. In order to be successful at failing, there must be an equal mixture of both. When they stand individually, they can be conquered. Together they are like the powers of Voltron.

Fear is defined as an unpleasant emotion that stems from the belief of danger being imminent. The emotion of fear is a common experience that is hard-wired in each of us. Its presence cannot be completely avoided. It is the emotion that sometimes balances life and death. In life, we witness situations daily that inform whether or not we are safe. Everyone wants to live at their perceived level of comfort. When that comfort is attacked, it emerges questions of what should be expected next. Fear is the result of the unknown potential.

One of my best recollections of a direct experience with fear still floats in my subconscious to this day. In my early twenties, I was going through an experimental phase with my voice. I had a group of friends that were actively pursuing music and had access to a recording studio. After one night of drinking and freestyling, they looked at me in amazement. Remember, I rarely shared my talents with others. No one really knew of my ability to come up with words and stories on the spot. All throughout the night, they kept urging me to join them in the studio to record something. This was around the time when Reggaeton was catching wind, and we wanted to follow that path. They were bilingual artists that had the ability to express themselves in English and Spanish fluently. They wanted to add me on as an additional element of diversity.

I was just beginning to recognize the power my voice possessed. Although I was experiencing these enlightenments, my confidence was still stifled in fully pursuing my purpose. Even with all of my hesitation, they were able to get me in the studio, and we recorded three songs. This was probably the freest I had ever allowed my words to be in public. I can remember the confidence that began to build after hearing my voice over powered studio monitors. That was probably this first moment I can recall believing what I had to say meant something. As we continued to work and have written and lyrical sessions, the background work was happening to develop a complete album. We sat down for business meetings to discuss promotion and distribution.

We seemed to be heading down a solid path towards progress. The discussion began to arise about going out and making our name known. This required securing performance platforms. Many people have had that gut-wrenching feeling that stagnates and reverses any progress ever made. At that moment, I positively did. I refused to express my fear to the group about actually getting on stage and performing. All of the hard work and commitment we dedicated could not go in vain. So as the planning continued, I sat in my nervous silence, hoping that this plan would not move forward. Well, it did.

I remember getting the phone call from the head honcho of this group we formed, Walter. He was the biggest pusher of me unleashing my talents. I can remember the energy in his voice when he told me that we secured a spot at this local nightclub to get on stage. I reminisce on him being so hype about us performing live, giving our music to the world. Still, I sat, refusing to show my nervousness and failing to confront my fear. I was mentally trying to push past it. But alone. I did not want anyone to try to help me through this. I was too embarrassed to tell anyone, especially those that did nothing but promote my esteem and confidence, that I was mortified by the idea of being on the stage.

I sat in my silence until our performance night. I can vividly remember battling my thoughts of following through. I finally built up enough courage to make a decision and go. I got dressed, hopped in my car, and drove to the club. When I arrived, the parking lot was packed. This was one of their hugely promoted nights. As I coasted through the lot, that pit of fear began to settle in my gut again. I pulled into a parking spot and just sat there, people watching. The more I sat, the more I started developing reasons why not going inside could be justified. To this day, I still look back with regret that I yielded the victory to those reasons. After sitting in my car for about twenty minutes, I made the firm to decision to drive off and go back home. The next day I heard from them about the success of the night. I still wonder what may have happened if I had walked into that club.

If fear is something innate to humans, why do we punish its presence? The immediate interpretation of fear is typically associated with some level of weakness or incapability. Rather it should be viewed as an opportunity to create bravery and courage. During that moment in the parking lot, I should have confronted my fear head-on. It should have been acknowledged and countered with success we accomplished to that point. The determining factor in its perception is the response to fear. If the reaction given does not create advancement to goals, then an internal investigation is in order.

The first task of investigation is to identify what is truly being feared. Placing an actual name and face to fear makes developing a defense technique become more direct. Is the face seen as a familiar one? If so, this means this obstacle has been physically survived before. Emotionally and mentally, maybe not so much. If this fear was defeated mentally, why has it returned? This frequently happens in life. The reason is that most people only look at the surface fear. Surface fear is when evaluating the current situation and how to get through it is only given. Preparation is not made to deal with similar issues down the road. We live life fearing the same thing over and over again but change nothing to address it. At some point, recognition must be given to the negative effects fear has on life. Is it worth experiencing those negative outcomes? Fear sometimes simply appears because we are being asked to endure experiences outside of our norm. The point that is commonly missed is we were not always in our comfort zone. The only way we got to a comfortable state was by exploring something unknown. This shows that we are granting the possibility to experience comfort at a much higher level by overcoming fear.

Having the strength to ask internal questions directed towards the presence of fear can be challenging. Fear can derive from direct and pseudo traumatic experiences. Our pseudo trauma comes from what has been witnessed through the paths of others. This is probably the most misleading reason for fear when looking at goal setting. This is equivalent to refusing tryout for the high school basketball team because a friend got cut. Sadly, there is a demographic of people that hold to this level of thinking. *It seemed impossible for someone else, so why should I try?* This is our automatic avoidance of pain.

What negative outcome are we expecting? Is this outcome something experienced before? If so, what went unconquered during the previous encounter? What is it about this event or action that makes goal achievement too terrifying to proceed? If the worst-case scenario does happen, is there a possibility of recovery? These are the questions that need to be self-directed. Fear only holds weight because we assume the possibility of damaging results if we follow through.

Preparation is probably the best weapon in the battle against fear. Proper planning is what provides comfort amid danger. Granted, all situations cannot be predicted, but the mindset can be strengthened. If severe mental anguish is frequent, what is being done to build the confidence needed to rise above? Take a moment to marinate in silent meditation. Keep an uplifting playlist of songs that can help push you through rough moments. Exercise more. Eat right. This list is infinite and is not one size fits all. The methods of perseverance differ for each individual.

Fear is created because situations are being observed through a singular view. Focus is only placed on the possible negative results. Remember, everything is dichotomous. If there are probable negatives, then there must be positive opportunities as well. To eliminate fear, possibilities must be identified just as clearly as setbacks. By looking at situations for good they may bring, hope is instantly developed. If pros outweigh cons, then theoretically, fear should not be a factor.

Fear can normally be easily conquered if one key factor remains unseen.

Doubt. This is the first cousin of fear from Wyoming. (No offense to any Wyomingites) Doubt comes around to ensure that fear feels comfortable. He is the cousin whispering reminders of how unsuccessful this plan could become. On the outside, doubt and fear hold a strong resemblance, but when a deeper look is given, the pain seated in doubt is much more critical.

If fear is the emotion experienced which delays progress, then doubt is the action. Doubt comes from a place of mistrust that was present long before the goal entered the mind.

Normally, doubt doesn't even have a direct relation with the achievement being pursued. Deep, unresolved pain from past life events gives doubt the ability to move freely in the mind. Somewhere in younger years, the belief of worthlessness was mentally implanted.

The formal definition of doubt is simply put as a feeling of uncertainty. Doubt, paired with fear, becomes tangible and presents itself loudly. When it is acted out, doubt shows no hesitation in expressing its stance. Whether shown verbally or physically, your surroundings will know when it has entered the room. Ignoring the pain that births doubt forces us to take actions that prevent stepping up. We do not enter the arena because of the pain endured to get to the other side.

What do we do instead? Excuses are created that make the ultimate goal less important. Unsuccessful stories that others have experienced begin floating through our mentality. Comparisons with unproductive people begin to justify our patterns. Placing ourselves on the same level as others diminishes our greatness. It kills our individuality.

It reminds me of those old black and white movies where the neighborhoods functioned on the same accord. Everyone has the same car. They work in the same factory. They leave for work at the same time. Every house and yard look the same. They come out to cut the grass at the same time of the day with the same type of lawnmower. This is what doubt mirrors. I am pretty sure that there is one individual in the neighborhood who saw an advertisement about a new lawnmower with all of the features they need. They want that lawnmower. It would be perfect for their individual life. The problem is they live in this neighborhood where different is frowned upon. Day after day, they think about the change that lawnmower would bring to their life.

So why don't they ever go buy it?

It starts with fear. The fear of being ridiculed by peers. Will I still be allowed in my social groups if I buy this lawnmower? Will people think I am being arrogant for breaking from the routine? The more fear is built towards being an individual, the more doubt is allowed to make moves.

The urgency of goals begins to fade.

The self-talk begins to focus solely on the negative outcomes that would occur if this lawnmower was purchased. *I bet it's just a fancy shell on a basic mower. Maintenance will be super expensive. It's going to cut grass just like my current lawnmower.* These doubting thoughts become persistent and repetitive.

We lose our nerve to follow through. Negative self-talk becomes the norm. Our body language begins to show tension and disappointment. Now every moment in the yard has to be masked with a facade. Smiling and waving at the neighbors but internally going through extreme hurt. We know that we could be having a better mowing experience.

How do we go about fixing this? How do we learn to overcome our fear and doubt? It all boils down to taking the correct actions. Fear and doubt have become so ingrained that it becomes impossible to change individual actions. This has become the norm, but no happiness is present. There is no peace.

In the aforementioned scenario, all that needs to be done to create happiness is to purchase the doggone lawnmower. That simple action will allow an immediate release of tension. There will be a resurgence of confidence. The decision to be unique enables the goal to get closer and celebration is in order. Regardless of the size of accomplishment, praise is worthy if there was progress. This confirms that the finish line is one lap closer than it was yesterday.

What is your lawnmower? What is the one thing needed in life that will instantly create improvement? Is counseling needed to address anger issues being battled that trickle into marriage or parenting? Does the road to entrepreneurship need mentoring to help ignite that idled business? It is time to start investigating and investing in personal behaviors.

Investigate by getting to the root of all internal issues. Look in the mirror and ask those tough questions. Confront the past demons. Then shift into investing in the change desired.

Some people may need to be removed from the circle. Finding a therapist may need to be a priority. Hone in on the skills needed to achieve the purpose. Do not fall into frustration because immediate change goes unseen. This is a process that will take time and effort.

Remember to ask if what is on the other side of the process is worth it. Will it provide the freedom the heart craves?

EPIPHANY

You know it's been a long time

Since I've sat and listened to my mind, think

Just sit back and enjoy a drink

Ease my head and cool my nerves

Understand and comprehend my thoughts and words

No more living life slurred

You know, having the ability to talk

But can't enunciate your verbs

Chris Daniel

Because the last time I heard

Those were labeled as action words

And in order to live life

continuous movement is vital in this world

This is why I come back

To the happiness of living life unslurred

Honestly, I was feeling like Langston

Having a 'Dream Deferred'

Knowing the direction but missing the turn

Following paths, I should not have learned

But I guess there comes a time

When everyone must feel the burn

WHEN DID YOU FIND YOU?

It's cool to sit back and watch the fire

But I bet there's a sting when it's your turn

Now once you get through

Just put Vaseline on the wound

Keep your head high and stern

Focus on what your heart craves and yearns

Because what's inside of you can never be taken

Unless you let it be withdrawn

Stand strong

Stop being someone else's pawn

Your dream will be guaranteed

Like dew at the breaking of dawn

And your new day will begin

So why not get out the bed

Open those blinds

And let your sunlight seep in.

Now that fear and doubt are out of the way, true work can begin. It is time to put boots on the ground and get active.

During the process of digging through fear and doubt, self-reflection was vital to improvement. The method does not change. As the journey to greatness begins, there will need to be a constant flow of reminders of the purpose. Remember, fear and doubt are not eliminated but only put in their proper place. On this road to greatness, there will always be new obstacles that will present themselves. These hindrances will not hold weight because the formula to overcome has already been discovered.

Self-reflection allows the opportunity to discover where the focus needs to be placed. Too many times, when trying to move on a goal, we start spinning our wheels. Do not confuse movement with progress. Many people look like they are working toward their goals because they seem so active. When results are closely reviewed, it is evident that they are in the same spot where they started.

When developing a plan, everything needs to be out on the table.

An itemized list should be developed to the most minuscule detail. This will allow the vision to organize what needs to be accomplished based on priority. If the goal is to be an author, it is senseless to spend day and night designing the book cover if writing has not started. Having a visualized idea is important, but the primary energy does not need to be there. Once the list is arranged, everything must be reviewed to identify what is necessary to complete each step. What resources will be required? How much time will need to be invested?

Once each tool has been acquired to travel forward, the hard part approaches. How to remain disciplined? How will the flame continue to be held to the feet to stay on the path? Who will instill accountability? Every dream chaser must have a solid support team. Environments need to be honest and blunt every step of the way. Accountability partners should be someone held in high regard. It must be a person whose opinions garner a lot of respect. If not, all of their advice will sound like criticism.

Building up external support will make it much easier to create internal inspiration. This is important because no matter how strong the team, they will not be present around the clock. Mental discipline must be possessed to hold self-accountability as well. These are the moments when fortitude will be tested.

Every day will not be a good day. There will not always be a success. It is okay. When these days are faced, reminders of the 'why' must be found. Own mistakes and learn from them. Gratitude must be found in the losses as much as it is in the wins. Losing allows the recognition of vulnerability. When a vulnerability is identified, strength can be developed. Everyone wants to be stronger, right? I always tell myself to make thousands of mistakes, just never the same one twice. Every experience is a learning moment. Once education is obtained, it is time to keep onward.

As the end goal gets closer, the dynamics of the support group will shift as well. Sometimes the people needed at the beginning phase cannot help in the middle or end.

This does not mean that they are now cut off indefinitely. Their role has just slightly changed. Instead of being in the starting five, they are with the second team off the bench.

Still an important piece, just not on the frontlines. When this shift occurs, it will allow the chance to decipher who is here for the long haul. Some may not feel comfortable coming off the bench. These players are not trying to get a championship with this team. They are here for the highlight reel and the ability to name drop. The only purpose they serve is to ride the coattails and make the burden heavier. When positions shift in the support group, it must be handled with grace.

In order to do so, humility should be seen at every level. If they are truly in the fighter's corner, there will always be a place somewhere. Do not humiliate those that must endure a shift in position for the sake of the greater good. Remind them of their value and allow them to see the impact of the new role. Many times, when the goal pursuer reaches a new level of success, it kindles a new sense of arrogance. They begin to walk around like it was all their doing. No help. This is how bridges get broken and bonds get destroyed. Everyone seeks appreciation. When gratitude fails to be given to those who have invested in this journey, resentment emerges.

Everyone deserves to be thanked along the journey to success. This applies to the critics as well as the fans. Thanks, must be given to the skeptics because they helped formulate the strength to conquer. Our ability to hear reminders of what may fail but still endure shows our power. The critics forced us to look inward and discover what it would take to make it. They gave us the blueprint to select the correct team for the mission. If it was not for the naysayer's, greatness may have never been attained. For this, they deserve a round of applause.

Should I have to explain why the fans receive the thanks? Who else was willing to hear your frustrations and still stick around? They stuck around when there was no evidence of fruition. Ultimate faith. They sent the uplifting videos and memes when it was nothing left inside. Their reasons for thanks are endless. Cue the standing ovation.

EVERYDAY

Life is such a precious blessing

That we all take for granted

Just the privilege to open your eyes

Makes us blessed by the Most High

No matter how much we try to deny

Forever will He stay on our side

Making sure that He provides

The tools needed to continue this ride

Chris Daniel

when we feel weak and torn inside

He lifts us towards the sky

giving that feeling of what it is to fly

Just like you

I've had dreams of making it in life

Lent my ears to the devil's advice

Most of the suggestions sounded nice

But we don't think of the sacrifice

taking the tempting over what's right

feeling in control of our days and nights

But how can we control

Something we did not create

WHEN DID YOU FIND YOU?

Why do your eyes blink?

Fingers bend and stomach ache

why are we here in this place?

Sounds to me like grace

What if things were reversed

And we weren't the ones who ruled Earth?

What if we were the ones

That lived and scrounged through the dirt?

What would be our worth

If animals were the ones

Walking, talking putting the inferior through hurt?

Would we view every day as a rebirth?

Chris Daniel

A chance to clear up yesterday's mistakes and errors

Not taking for granted our sunshine

Our breath, our love from others

Or the ability to love

Would we remove that need for hate?

Because we are too busy noticing

That we get to see them yet one more day

Understand that we are privileged and blessed

And that life

Is not to be constant pain and stress

Think of every morning as your best

challenge yourself and put others to the test

WHEN DID YOU FIND YOU?

To see if they are ready to accept

You giving everything you have left

to show them the love you possess in-depth

Anytime the thought of them was kept

I hope it is clearly understood there are people who did not wake up this morning. This is not a maybe or probably. This is a fact. Some people sat down yesterday and wrote out everything they were going to get done today. Some conversations needed to be accomplished. Goals that needed to be achieved. They laid their head on their pillow last night just knowing that it could all get done tomorrow.

I am not saying any of this to instill scare tactics. If anything, this should serve as a wakeup call to become active. I have heard some argue what is the point if death is inevitable.

I just shake my head. The point is legacy. Whether one is intentionally left or not, there will be a legacy left behind in your name. I can only speak for myself, but I want my name to continue as inspiration when I journey to the other side. I want my kids to hear my name and feel pride and motivation. I want them to know that everything that I did while breathing was to paint a picture of excellence.

We must wake up daily with an appreciation for our blessings. We get so wrapped up with intangible and material items that we do or do not have, and we lose focus.

The greatest gift that we will ever receive is the ability to open our eyes. Every time a new morning comes, it brings opportunity. Experiences encountered throughout the day are individually tailor-made. The good and the bad. Both are blessings that will facilitate growth.

The ill events of life teach valuable lessons only if there is a willingness to accept them. The most simple but essential lesson is learning what not to do. This message goes frequently missed because we get caught up in our emotions about the occurrence. It is okay to have emotions towards events but not to remain in them. When emotions sit, they block the view of new blessings and opportunities.

Emotions are designed to be temporary. They are simple reactions to stimuli. New stimuli brings new emotions. This is unless the skill of letting go of old emotions does not get mastered. This is not saying that everyone should be an emotionless person walking around numb. It is actually the contrary. Every emotion should be felt to its fullest extent. Here is the key though. Once the time has come to let it go, make sure it is let go.

Allowing emotions to sit and fester opens the door for inaccurate feelings down the road. Has an argument ever caused heavy feelings of anger because of hurtful things that were said? Have you ever allowed that anger to walk around with you all day? Has that anger interrupted every thought created during the day? Then all of a sudden, you walk into your favorite eatery only to learn they are out of your go-to dish. BAM. Immediately, everyone in the establishment gets cursed out. The inability to partake in that beloved dish definitely did not deserve this response level, especially if this is a frequented dining establishment. The anger given to the server is not actually directed at them. It may seem so in the moment, but it is just the opposite when deeper digging is done. This could have all been avoided had the original anger been handled. Refusing to address the emotions stemming from that argument now paint every scene as an attack against inner peace. This is when phrases like, *I'm not having a good day* and *the world is against me*, begin to verbalize.

This is completely untrue. Go back and pick apart the entire day. There is a high probability there was good sprinkled somewhere throughout. Even if many things do not go as planned, there are definitely bright spots. Appreciating blessings helps to recognize that time is not available to spend on anything outside of peace and joy. Just because anger is currently present does not mean that there will not be joy around the corner. The anger from that argument needed to be confronted right there at the moment. If the opportunity was not viable during the argument, it is your duty to reconcile inner peace. Taking ten minutes to sit down and breathe would allow freedom to truly explore what induced anger. Once the root is reached, it is discovered that the anger was only isolated to this situation. If the anger trigger stemmed from something deep in past experiences, it is imperative to find a way to heal that pain. Once the past pain can be pinpointed, energy should be shifted to rectification. No more misdirected anger. Now the day can be continued following a path towards peace and wellness. Make sure to call up the arguer later and explain the reasons for anger if needed. The key is to acknowledge the negative emotion and then keep moving forward.

Understanding that seeing a new day is a privilege demands gratitude. This is a reminder that there is something greater than us that is allowing another chance. Regardless of spiritual denomination or lack thereof, it is clear that life's enigma is greater than what any human can create. Since the beginning of time, the question of the purpose of life has been raised. The answer that I have lived believing is based on love and peace. These two elements are crucial to living a life that is more than just satisfactory.

When peace and love are absent from the equation, chaos runs free. Their archnemeses are hatred and distress. No one wakes up in the morning, excited to endure pain and hateful feelings. Although it may seem that way based on the cultural climate, it just is not so. People who live filled with anger and hate only subscribe to those feelings because peace and love were removed from them at some point. If they were constantly deprived, then the will to fight for it becomes diminished as well.

In order to outwardly show love, it must first be possessed within. If self-love shows to be incapable of manifestation, there is no way it can be given to others. Be careful allowing pessimistic voices, whether internally or externally, to build a nest of negativity. As mentioned earlier, meditation can be the ultimate key to finding that love for self.

Life moves so fast that it is not realized when self has been neglected. Many people I have approached about trying mediation seem unsure. Trust me, I understand. When I first started, I was skeptical as well. It has been sensationalized in the movies as this out-of-body experience that requires a bell and burning incense. Although that is possible, it is definitely not needed.

Mediation is just an opportunity to place the emphasis back on self. It does not have to be this long, drawn-out experience. Centering the mind, body, and soul can be done in sixty seconds. Our two most vital body organs, the heart, and lungs, move on a rhythm. They immediately respond when our body is out of sync. If we find ourselves under unnecessary stress, our hearts will begin to feel the pressure. When we are upset or agitated, it is sometimes hard to catch our breath.

This is because each individual walking on this Earth has

been given an internal soundtrack. The songs on our personalized playlist are unique to our advancement. It is impossible to plug in someone else's aux cord or download their app to hear your tracks. The same goes in reverse for anyone trying to plug into you. Their songs will be indiscernible. They will be audible but not make one ounce of sense. They will sound distorted and filled with static.

The problem is that this gets done every day. We all suffer from comparisons. At some point, everyone has looked at what others are doing and immediately felt bad about their position in life. The difference between people who achieve their goals and those who do not lie in one factor. The achievers do not live in comparison. They see what someone else is doing as motivation, not devastation. Comparison can cause obliviousness to the specialized soundtrack because someone else seems to be enjoying their songs more. There is no more energy being directed to the personalized playlist because the songs appear boring now. We do not understand that our soundtrack is like a Spotify Daily Mix. Repetitive listening will add new songs curated just for you. The only way to ensure the heart and lungs are taken care of is by cherishing the presence of interior love and peace. They are all intertwined.

Remaining humble is especially important when goal chasing. It keeps the soul grounded. Humility gets mistaken sometimes for this timid weakness that everyone should avoid. Quite the reverse. Humility requires a great deal of strength and willpower. To remain humble means being willing to fight off the temptation that will deter from the correct path. It is okay to enjoy successes and be proud. Hard work is supposed to be celebrated. The problem arises when we start to value our accomplishments over the journey.

Joy comes through the path we take to reach our success, not the materials we can receive. The lessons we learn. The relationships we build. If not for these things, there would be no success. If we lose gratitude for those, the material gains will not be as sweet.

When we start feeling above the relationships and lessons, it is a slap in their face and yours. Arrogance negates all of the energy placed in your dreams and the passion to keep going. Being humble comes from understanding that although we have reached a certain level, we are not spiritually above anyone.

Humility comes first from being a blessing to others. People refuse to follow this rule because they tie their blessings to monetary or materialistic value. Being a blessing for someone is nothing more than extending a hand when they seem down.

This can be done through passing knowledge, offering emotional support, or a good morning text. It makes no sense to build resources along the journey and then hoard them all.

Make sure that small mementos are kept as reminders of the

journey while traveling the path to success. If memories can always be associated with the origins, it becomes easier to appreciate the arrival. I once saw Ludacris on a social media platform showing off his 1993 Acura that he had long before things got *Fast and Furious*.

Sentimental reminders like this show achievement is possible as long as the will to fight lives. It is testimony that positioning in a low place is temporary and will not claim permanent residence. Every day the morning comes, arise and follow one simple routine.

Wake up. Understand you are a blessing. Give thanks for your blessing. Be a blessing to someone. Practice humility in every relationship and connection. If this routine is practiced consistently, the heart and lungs will remain filled with love and peace.

LATE NIGHT THOUGHTS

Since I can't go to sleep

On this paper, my pen must leak

Every time my eyelids meet

I think about every day I let life pass me

Like I was standing still at a track meet

The only things racing

Are the thoughts in my head saying

Chris Daniel

If you sit like this on your ass

You might as well be dead

Trying to talk myself into achievement

Although the spirit is in agreement

That this cycle can't be repeated

Being lazy in the flesh is all too convenient

The scenery is looking all too familiar

Different day same man in the mirror

Stress is pounding my mind

Could that be my breakthrough coming nearer?

The more fog in my sight

The more my vision gets clearer

Not another day do I want to hear

Of the money in my account disappearing

WHEN DID YOU FIND YOU?

What is a man that can't support his family?

Quite sorry if you ask me

And I'm not strictly talking financially

I plan to see my kids outstand me

Because I have shown how to stand and see

Themselves as an unlimited possibility

The first step in that is me

They will only learn based on what they see

If the picture I give them so vividly

Is to follow their dreams lazily and half-heartedly

Then they will get stuck in my same old seat

They must know how to handle defeat

And that is why at this point in my life

Giving up are words that I can never speak

Chris Daniel

Although my past haunts me

Taunts me into driving on that street

The only fuel my engine needs

Are the memories of what I was

Compared to the new me

Not a big, big difference

Just much more wisdom

I understand the mind can cripple and imprison

Any who allow themselves to be a victim

I am admitting

That I was once sitting

With a gun pointed to my dreams

Forcing my mind to start quitting

So easily could I have pulled that trigger

WHEN DID YOU FIND YOU?

Thank GOD, my faith was just a little bit bigger

For now, I see that big picture

Although my end date has been calculated and figured

My days until then will create all the difference

If you have made it this far through the book, congratulations are due.

If you have been taking notes on how to move closer to achieving goals, then a gold star is necessary. Now we are entering the Terror Dome. This is when suffering from some of the heaviest attacks will occur. Why?

Simply put, odds are being defied that haters thought would not be overcome.

In the beginning, they were throwing soft jabs and faints, knowing that chin was manufactured from glass. Now that hard work and training have been in place, a new type of fighter has developed. Those old punches will not work anymore. Now they are trying to throw only haymakers. True boxing fans know that is not good when going up against a skilled boxer.

The implementation of shell defense is impeccable now.

The punches can be read way before they are thrown. Stamina can now last 12 full rounds ten times over. The haters are stunned. They were not ready for this type of fight. This is not what they trained for. They were too busy focusing on old footage. When silence and focus on self are allowed, this is what happens.

Coming out better than ever is the only result, and no obstacle can stand in the way.

Now is definitely not the time to get lazy and think coasting through will accomplish something. The same training endured when you were lost in emotions is the same needed now. As stated over and over in this book, adversity is going to have a constant presence. The thought of letting off the gas is not welcome. This is the moment when that dog must be present internally. Mental toughness is what gets you to follow-through.

If at any point, giving up seems like the best option, it is time again to sit and self-reflect. Think of your starting point. Is that a place worth returning? Do you remember what it was like there? The pain. The hurt. The mental anguish. Is this needed back in your life?

In the last chapter, we discussed maintaining humility. This is where keeping those journey reminders can come in handy. They will serve as an acknowledgment of the mental freedom earned. Quitting now is like offering yourself to go back into bondage.

Opponents are going to try to send daily reminders of what was present in the past. They will try to convince that those times offer a better place. This is because you are no longer their punching bag. They are used to you getting punched and doing nothing about it. Sorry for all of the boxing references, but it is my favorite sport. Why, you ask? Probably because it is a perfect representation of life.

Boxing symbolizes an individual's fight to win at life. First, the opponent must be identified. Without that information, there is no way to train properly. It must be known who or what you are fighting to prepare accordingly. Once you know your fight, begin collecting resources to help ensure victory. Obtain the right equipment. Having the correct training facility and finding cornermen with expertise in the type of battle you are facing. Once the right tools are acquired, it is time to dig in.

Go dark. Remove every distraction and just train. During this process, make sure to get enough water. Make sure that dietary needs are restrictive and healthy. Speak to no one outside of the support group about the goals in pursuit. Your sparring partner is the most honest person in the group. They will go toe to toe with you, simulating the battle. They are willing to take punches because they know they are for a greater good. For them to be in this position, they must possess a certain level of strength, mentally and physically, essential to growth. Who else will understand that those punches are not coming from a place of anger? This is just a part of the process. Those are the friends and family members who understand when you may snap a little bit at them when things get slightly stressful. They will not take it personally. They will understand that was not really you going off on them. They will understand the pressure of the grind. Watch this though, as long as it is being done with humility. Do not just snap and leave it at that. Remind them it was all-out love and strictly because of the training.

After spending months in tunnel vision, the time for the big bout has come.

Time to get the entrance music and outfit ready for the show. You and the team make that slow walk to the ring. The announcer calls your name as you enter the canvas. The crowd goes wild, and your support team falls back. They are not out of reach but are unable to enter the direct battle with you. It is all on you and your training to determine if the goal is achieved. Ding-ding-ding-ding. The fight is on.

You are bobbing and weaving, landing some punches and taking some as well.

Combinations, uppercuts, jabs. The support team is still there watching diligently from the corner. At this point, they can only yell advice from the sidelines. They cannot enter the ring. It is all about muscle memory and the will to win. Each round gets tougher, and stamina gets tested. In between the bells, the opportunity to confer with the team on the sidelines becomes available. If you are messing up, they will let you know. If you are doing badly, they will let you know. It is crucial to take advantage of their advice during these times. They can see the whole view from the outside. Not only can they see the errors of the opponent but are observing your flaws as well.

In the real-life journey to greatness, you will get stumped and need outside information. There will come a point when relying strictly on internal knowledge will not be sufficient.

This is where the correct cornermen become important. If people in the corner are not qualified for their position, misinformation will be delivered, and a set up to be knocked out will be imminent. There are so many people working hard towards goals and wondering why they cannot get anywhere. Check your surroundings. If you have a cut man that does not know the correct angle to pressure the wound, it will bleed out. If your trainer does not know the proper routine needed to build stamina, exhaustion will arise by the third round. Friends that are around only for the ride and have nothing to contribute must go.

As the perseverance through the fight continues, there is one presence that cannot be ignored. No matter how irrelevant to the process, it cannot be overlooked. I'm talking about the crowd. The spectators. The audience. These people have no impact on success whatsoever. They will boo and cheer whether you or the opponent display triumph. You never know where these people will appear, but they will be easy to identify. This group will be composed of friends, family members, and those who have never even been met. These people will constantly offer their advice, whether good or bad but never offer means of getting it done. Their most common phrase is "I would have done_____if I were you". In sports, some refer to them as Monday morning quarterbacks. In life, you may hear them just be called backseat drivers. Whatever label is placed on them, it is imperative not to get comfortable with the sound of their voice. They are there for the confusion.

If they are congratulatory voices that are cheering but offering no goal support, they must also be muted. I am aware that they may mean well. They probably do not know how to offer the resources needed. That is understandable. What should not happen is getting wrapped up in their celebration. They are not fully aware of the end goal. They just see good and want to congratulate it. When we engulf ourselves with the cheers of small victories, we tend to become stagnant. We give ourselves that pat on the back like we have made it and tend to slightly let off the gas. Tell them to thank you, be appreciative, and keep moving forward.

If they are spewing noise of negativity, do not get trapped in a dispute with them. This is what they want. Distraction from the main goal. Anything that can be done to pull attention away from the path will be attempted. They see the good being produced but cannot figure out how to achieve it for themselves. This is their problem, not yours. The moment you get into a battle with them, their ego gets boosted. Your energy gets depleted. Your goals go unattained.

Perseverance is the key. Push through the adversity to reach the mountaintop. Just keep in mind how beautiful it will be once it is reached. Visualize being on top, receiving all of the fruits of labor.

STAY FOCUSED

Sometimes my thoughts should not be expressed

But the nonsense must be addressed

Can't save my words to ensure your comfortable nest

Anything on my mind must be removed from the chest

Attitude may be received because of your ignorance

But I refuse to hold on to the anger and stress

Whenever I do, I am never at my best

So, my true test

Chris Daniel

Is to stand over the mess

ensure it doesn't make any progress

I refuse to be defeated on my quest

Although I may stumble on my steps

I will always be at my best

So, to you, the only thing I can suggest

Is to keep your eyes on your test

Because my answers may not be correct

And even if they are

Your effort would be meaningless

Because instead of working hard for your success

You rode my shoulders

WHEN DID YOU FIND YOU?

Without them, you are powerless

So as your journey continues, remember this

Follow your own path

Before you get caught in my mess

As I chase success, I think sometimes, is it truly worth it? Should I put in all of this effort for something that I am not so sure about? Although my answer remains yes, I wonder why I haven't made it. Every morning that sunlight touches my eyes, I am thinking about what needs to be done for me to move forward. Somehow it doesn't get done. It finally hit me one day. I know that I possess the capability to attain high levels of success.

The doubt that sits within is the ability to maintain it consistently. Do I have the stamina to continue? If I don't, what will happen to all of my hard work? What will happen to those who now depend on my grind?

As soon as I impose those questions to myself, I get a wake-up call. A reminder that my voice was not built to be silent. Speaking personally, that is the gift that was given to me. How selfish would I be not to share it? Just think of when you are receiving gifts on Christmas or your birthday. The desire to show them off is boiling over with exhilaration. You are ready to sport that new outfit. Spray that new cologne or perfume. Get behind the wheel of that new car. It should be the same with the God-given talents that were designed specifically for you.

If it has not been done already, weed out the last few haters still lingering in your direct circle. For those hating outside of the circle allow them to do what they do. Be sure to make it clear that it cannot be done in your presence, though. Time is up for sitting in silence as they launch their attacks. If this book's advice has been insightful, there should now be a well-oiled routine that positions you steps ahead of the haters. Be willing to unapologetically tell them the truth.

Remember, there is no more fear. No more doubt. The opposition does not have the ability to knockout anymore. You know your full potential. It is now conceivable to confidently voice up to the haters. Let them know avidly that their negativity no longer holds any place in the mission. I do not care who it is. It can be parents, close friends, teachers, bosses, or spectators from the nosebleeds. They no longer have any dominion over your goal. You have reclaimed your power.

They have spent their entire time trying to implement their infiltration and inconvenience the plan. Now it is time to deliver that in reverse. It is now your turn to infiltrate their hatred with success. This is Kryptonite to any hater. The best thing being done to remove their validity is attaining success. Remember, the goal of the skeptic is to knock you far off the desired path so that they can illuminate themselves. As long as everyone around them is doing badly, their mission is achieved. Every time you rise above their attempts and keep on the path, the reduction in negativity occurs. This shows that amid adversity, success will arrive.

I know that it is difficult to remove some skeptics from view, especially if they are parents or close loved ones. I hope that their true love will allow them to see why it is impossible to accept their pessimism. Hopefully, as you continue to grow and achieve new successes, they receive clarity in their thinking errors. Proving them wrong through achievements will force them to look inward to see where that cynicism is derived.

If the strength to address these people is not found, you will be placing yourself back at square one. Not being able to trust and use your voice creates more pain and hurt. Let the weight go. We already know that more adversity is coming. Why hold on to the old? Develop a solution. Apply that solution. Move forward. The heavier the burden will be if the choice is not to let go.

Is the internal question of how to stay positive when the certainty of challenges is present being asked? Continue to self-reflect. Those same strategies that were used to eliminate initial fears and doubts must be continued. If you were waking up each morning to meditate and exercise, continue. If you found yourself taking daily rides just to clear your mind, continue. Journaling? Continue. Any strategies used to ensure peace should forever be implemented. Progress is not composed of a one and done remedy. Remember where you were when you started this. Remember how difficult the struggle was while dealing with past pain and no goals achieved. Now that some advancement has been made, it is more of the reason to dig your heels in and keep walking.

This is why many athletes do not reach their pinnacle. This is why some businesses close down before their time. Many people reach the summit of struggle mountain and get so wrapped in celebration they forget there are more mountains ahead. A granted celebration is necessary but must not overcast the fact that advancement is still required. Think of our children. Once they learn the alphabet, do they stop there? We applaud their achievement but also know that now it is time to move on to learning words. From words, we go to sentences and then on to paragraphs. As they keep advancing, they build the knowledge needed to share their story. Life is a process of forever learning. If no dedication is given to moving forward at every step of life, residence in an underground casket may be necessary. I did not mean to go dark there, but it is true. I always pose this question: Are you living life or just living to live? Are you chasing your potential to the fullest or doing just enough to get a passing grade on the test?

In order to ensure that the highest grade in life is being

pursued, three things must be done. Prepare. Persist. Produce. Preparation allows a view of the storm approaching. It gives time to gather all of the resources needed to survive. Use time wisely during the preparation stage because sitting around twiddling thumbs as if the storm will cease its approach is pointless. Proper planning allows room for contingency plans in the event that the storm takes a shift. A lot of times, we plan only thinking of positive and predictable outcomes. We block thoughts towards the obstacles that may arise. No one wants to think about how they may fail. I do not look at it as focusing on possibilities of failure. On the contrary, planning with exigence ensures that there will always be a path to the goal. It speaks to resiliency and determination to accomplish what has been started. Remember, there is no control over how strong the storm may become, only how you choose to react.

Once all of the primary resources are collected, it is time to hunker down and endure the storm. Persistence is vital here. This is not the time for panic. The storm will create thoughts of not making it through. You will feel the walls shake from the thunder. Trees may fall into the yard from the lightning. Your clothes will get wet, and shoes will become muddy. Have faith in the preparation. Trust the process. When obstacles jump on the path, it does not change the location of our destiny. The ultimate goal is still in the same place. You just have to figure out what needs to be shifted to get there. I tend to view goals like they are sunshine. Everyone wants to experience a bright, sunny day, Unfortunately, not all days give that luxury. There will be rain, clouds, and thunderstorms. This does not mean we will never see a sunny day again. The sun stays in its same spot. It never moves. No matter how many grey clouds form, the sun will return. When we lose sight of that, we panic and make decisions that take us further away from our sunshine. There is never a good time for panic but definitely inappropriate amid a storm.

If the first two steps are followed thoroughly, the product of the aftermath will flourish greatly. These are the fruits of our trees. This builds confidence to go out and do more. Just recall for a second how great it felt internally when a goal was accomplished. No matter if the goal was grand or minuscule, there was a sense of pride that sat within. The anticipation to share results with the world could not be contained. No one completes a task without wanting some level of recognition and acknowledgment. Also, think of the weight that is now lifted. All of the time spent wondering if it could be done, and now it is known that it clearly can. This also helps in your path to the next goal. Yes, the next goal. The average life expectancy is near 78 years. There is no way that amount of time can be spent on Earth to only chase one goal. Now that the formula has been developed, it can be applied to anything the heart desires.

Now is the time to engage in celebration. Remember not too much, only what is necessary. We do not want to get comfortable and forget there is still more work to be done.

Once you are granted the freedom that your goals give, spend time enjoying life. It has been earned. Whatever celebration looks like, bring to mind that it is well deserved. This could range from taking that life trip you have always envisioned to playing with your children more.

Remember, the game of life is chess, not checkers. You cannot just freely jump around the board with no plan or strategy. In checkers, every piece is looked at the same until you make it to the goal. This is not how life works. There is not a cookie-cutter design that will work the same for every goal. There are multiple pieces on the board, and each one is designed for a specific function. If you are not thinking five steps ahead, you will find yourself in a trap. All of the pieces in your life are necessary according to their purpose. You must be surrounded by a strong front so that your kingdom, state of mind, does not fall victim to attack or capture. Organize. Strategize. Claim victory. Checkmate.

GRATITUDE

I would like to extend a huge THANK YOU for taking the time to read my thoughts. This is my very first published book and it means a great deal to have hopefully blessed someone. The transition to completion has taken the utilization of every concept mentioned. I officially began writing this book around 2015 but could never hold myself accountable to finishing. Although I knew what needed to be done, I allowed every excuse to get in the way of my destiny. The year 2020 gave me no other choice but to sit down and let God guide me to my purpose. It was definitely a struggle to be obedient and follow His every direction. The obstacles that kept emerging had me doubting the mission at times. The more time I was given to sit without distractions allowed me the ability to realize majority of those challenges were self-inflicted. Once I was granted enlightenment it became imperative to refuse permission for the mind to be greater than the Spirit. I pray this book was able to provide the same level of insight. We are all designed for greatness. However, it can only be accomplished when we accept that our path may not look as initially envisioned. The key is regardless how many alternate routes the journey offers, continue to stay true to self. I hope that everyone who read these words can one day answer the question, When Did You Find You?

Author's Page

CHRIS DANIEL

Chris Daniel is a native Houstonian with a unique passion for words. Ever since a youth, he has understood the impact verbalized and written communication can have in life. His infatuation with words was ignited by the universal language of music. It was clear to Chris that music had the ability to touch the soul with a force much greater than normal conversation could compare. His childhood was flooded with rhythmic sounds at every corner. The lyrics that created harmonious stories told from a variety of perspectives encouraged him to view life through a different lens. As Chris continued to grow in age, his own life experiences developed a deeper connection with music. It allowed him an avenue to explore self-insight regardless of the origin of genre.

The self-awareness music created inspired Chris to seek a Bachelors of Science in Psychology from Texas Southern University. It was during his collegiate years when he began to hone his gift with words. A basic love for poetry writing began to flourish into a means of therapeutic balancing. He began working in education while still moonlighting as a writer and spoken word artist. He put every piece of energy in being an outstanding secondary teacher. His time in the classroom roused realization that his calling to connect with students was greater than the confines of lesson plans and TEKS focused curricula. This calling led him to pursue his second degree, earning a Master's in School Counseling at the University of Houston-Clear Lake. In his years of counseling the adolescent future, which he still currently does, he never allowed his ink pen to dry. His love for music continues to drive his counseling techniques as well as writing style. He is truly InLove with Words.